'ARRY THE AARDVARK

AN' 'IS PALS

Written and Illustrated by

MARTIN CONWAY

For Mary
from Martin
To Inspire you!

ISBN-13: 978-1544812021
ISBN-10: 1544812027

Dedication

To my wife Soraya for all her support and patience

CONTENTS

'ARRY AN' 'IS 'OME

'Arry the Aardvark, that's right, that's 'is name'

Lives in an 'ole in the ground on the plain.

An 'ole for 'is 'ome, I can 'ear you all think,

Can't be much of a thing, for an 'ome it must stink.

But an 'ole in the ground

Is where Aardvarks is found,

In a big deep burrow...

Oh, your brows in a furrow....

Is a burrow an 'ome

Or an 'ome a Gnome

An is Nome in Alaska

I've jus' gotta ask ya?

An yes in the ground is where burrows is made,
Great big 'oles in the soil
Made by lots of 'ard toil.
An' dug with no spade,
(Would make 'Arry's blood boil)

Cos an Aardvarks got claws
An' very strong paws
What for diggin' are great things
Doin' big 'oles on them plains.

An Aardvarks is proud of their 'omes mus' be said,
The soil's all packed 'ard with soft grasses for bed.
For an 'ome wot's not clean is no good for none,,
Not least for an Aardvark jus' in from the 'unt.

So they sleep there by day, out of the 'ot sun,
Till at night they goes out, for the 'unt or for fun.
Or in the cool evening to sit an' relax,
With the sights an' the sounds from Lions to Bats.

AARDVARKS DON'T SWIM

'Arry the Aardvark an' Joe the Giraffe
Was watchin' an Elephant 'avin' a bath.
Now 'avin' a bath is a very fine thing,
Especial' fine if as well you can swim.

But if you can't swim then you're makin' a gaffe,
Givin' the locals an' 'oot o' a laugh.
Now Aardvarks an' water don't mix very well,
They prefer dust baths best we can tell,

For drinkin' then water is jus' fine an' dandy,
A swim's best avoided unless things go badly.
An' Joe with 'is long legs would never go down,
In case in the water he'd sink an' might drown.

That very thought makes our 'Arry's 'ead ring,

Oo' would be minded to do such a thing?

Grassland an' 'ills is where Aardvarks do best,

'Untin' by night fer a nice termite nest.

Giraffes they needs trees to be at their ease

An' don't like no water up over their knees.

Rollin' in mud is fer 'ippos' an' others,

Much too 'ard fer Aardvarks to be bothered.

Oo' wants to be soakin' an' covered in mud

When a roll in the dust is so good fer your mood?

'ARRY AN' THE CLOUD

Now 'Arry n' Barry n' Gary n' Larry

Was standin' far out on the plain.

They was watchin' a cloud in the distance far off,

An' at first they all thought it was rain.

But the cloud moved so fast,

And what's more did not last,

That real puzzled they looked once again.

Cos unknown to them

The cloud on the plain

Was in fact not the rain,

But the smoke from a fast moving train.

It was 'Arry first spoke

To the rest of the blokes,

As e' tried not to choke,

(From the shock, not the smoke),

"Now I've seen many things
In my winter's n' springs,
But a cloud that's so low
An' so fast as it goes,
An' that doesn't leave rain
As it crosses the plain,
Is a thing wondrous rare
That I've no words to spare..."

An all that bein' said
Sweat sprang from 'is 'ead,
These words were too many,
The sight too uncanny.
For standin' is one thing an' talkin' another,
An' lookin's a fine thing an' thinkin's no bother,
But even 'Arry was reelin'
When all were together,
Cos it's 'ard fer an Aardvark when out on the plain,
It's 'ard to do more'n one thing.

'ARRY AN' THE ELEPHANTS

'Arry an' Larry stood by a rock,
Watchin' some Elephants out for a walk.
They was tall round an' red
With the dust from the plains,
And they swayed as they trod
Through grass yellow and green.

Said Larry to 'Arry
"Well, I am amazed,
I mean 'ow many termites
Gets ate in a day!
'Ow much does it take 'em
To fill up their tums?
Two or three 'mite 'ills,
An' that's goin' some!"

Says 'Arry to Larry,

"Oh mate, no, no, no!

Them's got a big nose

But no 'mites up there goes.

It's leaves wot they eats

From the bushes 'n' trees,

Ants, bugs, 'n' termites

Would jus' make 'em sneeze."

Larry amazed looked at 'Arry again,

Was there nowt 'e don't know

About things on the plain?

Our 'Arry 'e' nods in a knowin' sort o' way,

Cos learnin's a thing you don't learn in a day.

'ARRY AN' THE NIGHT SKY

'Arry an' Larry out on their backs
On a big flat rock in a grassy patch.
The night was dark an' the sky was clear,
The Moon cast shadows far an' near.

Says Larry, "Well Arry, wot does it mean
All that up there where none 'as been?"
"Now that mate," says Arry," is a very good question,
An' I won't give an answer jus' by guessin'.

There's things as we knows of,
There's things as we don't 'cos
We're 'ere to eat termites,
An' 'unt out on dark nights,
To walk out on the grass
An' watch Wildebeests' pass.

We can dig out our burrows,
Won't make our brows furrow
Unless we go thinkin'
'bout things up there blinkin'."

Larry then nodded, agreein' jus' some,
With these words of wisdom
As from 'Arry 'ad come.
Oo' else amongst Aardvarks
Could use all them smart words?
Bar 'Arry, course, 'e could,
'is discourse bein' so good,
'is mind right on track, 'e was sharp as a tack,
For an Aardvark as sharp as a tack.

'ARRY AN' THE OLD CAR

'Arry the Aardvark came across an old car,
Far out in the grasslands where few people are.
"Now what might this 'ere be?" 'e asked of 'imself
As 'e stood in the shade of a small rocky shelf.

"I jus' might 'ave to go out an' see this more clear,
Cos it jus' 'asn't moved since the time I was 'ere."
So after an hour or it might 'ave been four,
'Arry was close to the car's open door.

He pondered a while cos decisions come 'ard,
To an Aardvark alone where they concern a car.
"What kind of beast was this then?" he thought,
"That can lie 'ere so still even though it's so hot.
It might jus' be awaitin' an Aardvark like me,
Go too close to it's teeth so's it can 'ave tea"

Then after a while and a little while more,

'Arry backed off from the wide open door.

It was 'ard to decide what 'e should do next,

But food an' a rest seemed a very good bet.

'ARRY AN' THE STRANGE CRITTER

'Arry the Aardvark was 'avin' a laugh,
Wi' 'is mates 'e' was 'avin' a laugh.
They was laughin' so 'ard
That they ran out of puff,
An' was flat on their backs,
Laid out on the green stuff.

An' why, you might ask,
Was they laughin' so fierce?
That they couldn't be tasked
Jus' to stand on their feet?

Well, they'd jus' seen a critter,
A two legged creature,
Was tall an' was gangly
An' 'orrid of feature,

With one huge big eye

Fillin' most of its face,

On a big shiny 'ead

Never seen in this place.

Was none like they'd seen

Any time in their lives,

They could laugh or could cry,

Or could run off an' 'ide,

But the laughin' that day

Is what felt jus' quite right!

'ARRY DIGS AN 'OLE

Down at the water 'ole on the 'ottest o' days,

'Arry an' Larry found the water away.

All round the 'ole other animals stood,

All lookin' worried, this was not good.

'Arry an' Larry looked one at the other,

An' to a big ol' root they both walked together.

An' there in the shade there was mud that was soft,

Where 'Arry an' Larry dug fast with their claws.

An' after a while, the mud still was flyin',

Of a sudden the water around them was lyin'.

Quite soon from a puddle a big pool was formin',

Where all o' the animals soon got to drinkin'.

'Arry an' Larry soon both 'ad their fill,

An' walked 'appily on, to the next termite 'ill.

'ARRY AN' THE FLOOD

'Arry the Aardvark stood 'igh on a rock,
Wi' 'is mates all around 'im below.
The rain 'ad bin fallin' fer hours an' hours,
Wi' no sign that it was goin' to slow.

Away on the plain, at the edge o' the trees'
Flood waters were edgin' much closer,
Even quite near it was up to the knees
Of Gnu oo' were movin' to shelter.

"It's plain to be seen", says 'Arry to all,
"We jus' cannot stay 'ere no longer".
They nodded as one as our 'Arry stood tall,
'Is wisdom a thing of great wonder.
"So pack up your gear an' we'll move a bit 'igher,
Up to the 'ills over yonder."

As 'e pointed more Northern

The lads took to wondrin'.

The move they was makin'

'Ad never been taken

By any Aardvark still on the plains then,

An' some felt a thrill

'Bout a life in the 'ills,

But others was ill an' was shakin'.

"Don't worry my friends, all will be well,"

Says 'Arry from where 'e is stood.

"We'll dig our new burrows, all fresh and new,

Lined with grasses we'll pick at the woods.

"Now let us be goin',

The waters' still comin',

We all need to get us some food.

Then we'll be walkin', then talkin', then diggin',

One thing at a time, which is good."

For as Aardvarks will tell you when things is goin’ rough,

Doin’ one thing at a time is mostly enough,

For an Aardvark it’s plenty enough.

'ARRY AN' THE EARTHQUAKE

'Arry 'an Larry 'an Barry 'an Gary

'Ad been out all night in the 'ills.

They'd been 'untin' till light,

They was lookin' fer mites,

'An 'opin' to 'ave of their fill.

When all of a sudden

With no kind of warnin',

In a great noisy rush

'An of shakin' 'an dust,

The 'ole earth was movin'

In a strange kind of groovin'.

The lads they was wobblin'

'An swayin' 'an bobbin',

As their feet seemed to move on their own.

Their ears were all ringin'

Their 'eads were all spinnin',

They wobbled like jelly from skin down to bone.

As sudden it stopped

The boys found they could walk,

Things was all normal again.

Our 'Arry said,"Surely, as sure as we's 'ere

Nothin' like this 'as been seen lads fer years.

We'd best be off 'ome 'an don't take too much care,

Was so odd it can't 'appen again, never fear.

'ARRY AN' THE GREAT BIRD

'Arry the Aardvark an' some o' the boys
'Was standin' aroun' an' not makin' no noise,
Cos' noise isn't somethin' that Aardvarks much like,
It makes their 'eads ache well into the night.

So quiet was they, as they stood contemplatin'
All o' them termites that soon they'd be eatin'.
When all of a sudden, in a great noisy rush,
A huge bird flew over like they would be crushed.

So they dived one an' all to the 'ot an' 'ard ground,
As the great shinin' bird disappeared in its sound.
No bird by an Aardvark 'ad ever been seen
As big or as fast as 'ad that one just been.

An' the boys all stood up, their 'eads all a shakin',

As 'Arry said "Ome lads, cos my ears is ringin'."

So off they all walked in a slow steady file,

All thoughts of termites now gone for a while.

Instead they was thinkin' of tales they would tell,

Of 'ow on one evenin' a great bird 'ad fell

On them down below as for food it did seek,

But found only brave Aardvarks oo's not quite so meek,

Oo fought long 'an 'ard, an' oo' finally won,

An' chased off the great bird at settin' o' sun.

'ARRY 'AS A CLOSE CALL

'Arry the Aardvark stood starin' right up,

Thankin' 'is stars fer a good piece o'luck.

'E was starin' right up at Joe the Giraffe,

Oo's big feet 'ad jus' missed 'im in the long grass.

Joe an' our 'Arry went back quite a ways,

'Avin been born on the very same day.

Joe says to 'Arry,"Sorry wee man

Eatin' Acacia leaves was my plan,

I missed you because I'm up here so high,

An' you're not exactly the tallest of guys!"

"S'ok," says 'Arry, "I quite get the point,
Not bein' even as 'igh as yer lowest knee joint.
It's 'ard fer an Aardvark out on this plain,
But bein' squashed by a pal would be a real pain."

So 'Arry curled up at the base o' the tree,
'E needed 'is rest after talkin', you see.
'E'd wait until dark an' be on 'is way,
Catch ants as they finished their work o' the day.

An' after a good feed o' ants an' some grubs,
'E'd stretch on the grass an' 'ave a good rub.
Then back to the burrow to sleep once again,
Till the next day was gone an' evenin' 'ad came.

JOE THE GIRAFFE TAKES A DRINK

As 'Arry was sittin' out 'avin' a think

'E saw 'is mate Joe come down for a drink.

For Joe the Giraffe, oo's a really tall feller,

Gettin' a drink from the pool

Is real 'ard, 'e will tell yer.

So long are 'is legs,

An' 'is neck jus' the same'

That 'e' can't reach the water

In the way that 'e' oughter.

So to get 'is 'ead down

Fer the drink that 'e' needs,

'Is legs 'e' spreads out

Till 'is mouths near 'is knees.

An' with a push a bit 'arder

'Is 'ead reaches farther,

Till 'is tongue can reach down

To the pool cool an' brown.

An' 'e' sooks an' 'e' sooks

An' the water goes up,

All the way up 'is neck side

Till it reaches the top,

Then it goes down

On 'is long an' deep insides,

An' as it goes down

'Is belly fills up,

Until Joe is 'appy

An' slowly stands up.

THE BIG AARDVARK

Stood 'igh on a rock with the sun at 'is back,

'E cast a long shadow deeper than black.

A shadow so big 'e could nearly not track,

'E must be the biggestest ever Aardvark!

Off to the side in the shade of the stone,

Our 'Arry was watchin' as Barry dreamed on.

E'd stood there 'isself as a boy an' 'ad thought

That never an Aardvark so big would be sought.

Until one time 'is Dad 'ad called out with a shout,

An' 'is dreams of such greatness 'ad all come to nowt.

So let the young dream,

It don't do no 'arm.

There'll be time to come down

When they're full old 'n' grown.

JILL THE GAZELLE

Jill the Gazelle an' some o' her ilk

Was out runnin' an' boundin' like they always will.

They leapt over rocks an' bushes an' mounds,

An' flew over 'Arry an' 'is mates on the ground.

They was obvious 'avin' a whole lot of fun

Though 'ow in that 'eat could they so fast to run?

An' yet there they was, bouncin' 'igh, goin' fast,

Ziggin' an' zaggin' as quick as a flash.

Jus' watchin' got 'Arry an' 'is mates all unsorted,

So they lay back down for a nap quite exhausted.

BUFFALO BILL

Buffalo Bill, well wot else would you call 'im?
Was down in the pool an' was 'avin' a wallow.
'E saw 'Arry an' Larry 'oo were jus' stood a watchin'
An' called them to join 'im where it was shallow.

"No thanks Bill", said 'Arry,"we'll jus' take a pass,
We Aardvarks an' water jus' wouldn't last.
Swimmin's not somethin' we's quite used to doin',
We're 'appy wi' dust baths 'cos our fur don't get ruined."

"Pity," said Bill, "'cos the pool's really fine,
An' in 'ere we Buffalo spend lots of our time,
Then when we're clean an' we look at our best,
We wallow in mud for to keep off the pests."

GIRAFFES IS TALL FELLERS

Out on the plain a Giraffe 'erd was walkin',

An' 'Arry an' Larry an' Barry stood starin',

At the sight of these fellers

With long legs like pillars,

Wot went up an' up,

Not seemin' to stop,

To a neck just as long

With an' 'ead up on top.

An' they walk kind of slowly,

But the ground that they go by

Seems to go very quickly

Their steps is so big eh?

"Wouldn't like to be that tall,

Wouldn't like it, not at all,"

Says 'Arry to them all,

Says 'Arry says 'e.

"Couldn't make me a burrow,

Would take more'n tomorrow

To make a good burrow

To fit one o' these.

We'd always be diggin',

Not stoppin' nor eatin',

Jus' diggin' an' diggin'

An' very, very deep.

But at the end o' the day,

One thing I can say,

That when all goes their ways, they would really really sleep."

ZEB THE ZEBRA

Zeb the Zebra was staring around,

From his not quite so high spot close to the ground.

He could see lots of bellies, stripey and round,

But no part of his Mum could he see to be found.

Trying to spot his Mum in the crowd,

Not a bit of her stood out clearly and proud.

So he entered into the black and white masses,

That were moving along in the tall waving grasses,

And shouted out long, and loudly, and clear,

"Mum, if you hear me, please come and be near!"

And all of a sudden, through the crowd shoving,

There was his Mum, with his sister and cousins,

Calling his name, saying "Stay where you are,

And now that we've found you, please don't go so far!"

THE HIPPO

I've got a big, big mouth with big, big teeth,

I weigh two tons but can still run at speed.

When I jump in the water it all splashes over

Whoever is standing too close.

Then I sink to the bottom and off I go running

Then pop up just to my nose.

I look all around 'til I see what's goin' down,

Well, that would be me of course.

I'm a hip hippopotamus

So roll with the lot of us,

But just watch that you don't get squashed

'Cause we're round and we're fun

We weigh in at two tons

So be careful that you don't get squashed.

'ARRY GIVES ADVICE

Said 'Arry to Larry, oo 'ad a crease in 'is brow,

"Don't 'urry wee pal, it won't do good no how.

When you've got a worry don't be in 'an 'urry,

When you're in 'an 'urry it jus' makes the worry

Come quicker towards you, the worst thing you could do.

Slow right down your thinkin',

Take time for the plannin'

Wot needs to be doin'

So as you don't ruin

The rest of your forenoon."

Then 'Arry sat down slow,

Sweat on 'is 'ot brow showed

From all of the effort

Of talkin' with no stop.

Our Larry stood awed

'An amazed 'an agog

At the genius before 'im

Oo knew all things worth knowin'.

Was there ever an Aardvark abroad in the land

As smart as was 'Arry oo led the Plains Clan.

'ARRY GOES QUIETLY

'Arry our pal was out on the 'unt
In the cool of an evenin' breeze.
It rustled the grass
On which stood the Giraffes
And it shivered the leaves
Of Acacia trees.

Now 'Arry was still,
'Cos 'e'd spied some Hyena,
An' that could bode ill
For there's not many meaner.
So still did 'e stand
Until night took the land.

Now feelin' some braver,
As e's the best o' night 'unter's,
Our 'Arry's back nearer
Where Hyena's still mutters.

Then quiet 'e passes

'Is way in the grasses,

An' stirs not a one

Until 'e 'as gone.

'Arry the Aardvark was back on the plain,
'E jus' 'ad to check out the car thing again.
'Course 'Arry did not 'ave a clue about cars,
This bein' the first 'e 'ad seen near or far.

'E stood by the rock shelf an' 'ad a wee think,
To save 'im from movin' 'e did not even blink.
For the thinkin' is 'ard, very, very 'ard indeed,
Too 'ard for most Aardvarks unless there's great need.

And of course such a beast as 'e saw in the grass
Was a worryin' thing to all 'oo might pass.
Why was it 'ere an' what was it doin',
Scarin' good Aardvarks from where they was goin'.

In time after thinkin' our 'Arry went close,
As 'e looked 'e was sure the beast's mouth wasn't closed.
It's huge red teeth in a line lay bared,
An' yet not a sound or a growl could be 'eard.

Now 'Arry's the bravest of Aardvarks is 'e,
An' boldly 'e steps to the big silent beast.
'E stands there a lookin' close at its great bulk,
But there's no sound or movin' it might be an 'ulk,

After a while and a while and some more,
When 'Arry 'ad pondered what 'e stood before,
'E set off for 'ome an' some food an' 'is bed
For too much 'ard lookin' was doin' in 'is 'ead.

GNORA THE GNU

Gnora the Gnu is a good lookin' gal,

So she was told by her Gnu wee pal.

Now her pal wasn't new,

Just that she was a Gnu,

So she wasn't a new pal,

Just a Gnu pal.

She has more than just one pal

For Gnu are quite social,

And in any one locale

Which Gnu have made focal,

There are not one or two Gnu,

But thousands or mores true.

They move always together,

In sun or wet weather,

On the plain or the river,

The herd their protector,

From Cheetahs' fast running,

Or Lion packs hunting.

And in there among them

Might Gnora be found,

Her friends, and there's many,

All circling her round.

The news among Gnus'

That she's going to be Queen,

As the best looking Gnu

That there ever has been.

LOUSY

When 'Arry 'an Larry was out at the 'ills,

Eatin' o' termites an' 'avin' their fill,

Larry of a sudden withdrew out 'is snout,

Sayin' "Wot was that then, wot's that about."

For 'stead o' a 'mite,

A nice tasty bite,

E'd sucked up a louse

Right up to 'is mouth,

An' it wasn't real nice,

No not at all nice,

Wot with 'undreds o' legs

An' a back 'ard to crack.

It was not wot you'd 'spect

The wrong kind of insect,

On an evenin' like that in the 'ills.

ZONKY THE ZEBRA TAKES A WALK

Zonky the Zebra stood by a Rhino with its long and pointed horn,

She next met an Elephant, big round and grey, with a nose so very long,

On big flat feet it swayed its way in the light of the early dawn.

Zonky saw Cheetahs' stretched out on a mound,

Scanning the whole of the land all around.

They are oh so fast, so she took off and hid

In the low lying ground behind some dead wood.

A tall neck appeared with a head on the end,

As Mister Giraffe went out to meet friends.

She went down by the water-hole to see the Gazelle,

They were milling around at the edge of the pool.

When a lion roared loud they went off as a crowd,

Bounding high in the air looking cool.

Hyena were laughing as Zonky was thrashing

Her way through the thick green bush.

She hurried along, for avoiding their song

Was also avoiding their tooth.

Gnu were out grazing, vast herds quite amazing,

Taking off in a great dusty run,

And Zonky stood watching, but not joining in,

She was not at all sure with Gnu's it was fun.

Then she could see across by some trees,

A pattern she knew all at once.

Tearing along she was soon safe ensconced,

And with the herd she then blended for lunch.

'ARRY THE AARDVARK AN' THE GNU'S NAMES

'Arry the Aardvark started to talk,

But 'e didn't walk, only to talk,

Cos it's 'ard for an Aardvark to talk an' to walk

Or to talk an' to walk, it's 'ard.

Says 'Arry to Barry now 'is thoughts were in train,

"Ad a real bad experience out on the plain,

Saw a really big 'erd o' them Gnu yet again,

You know 'em Baz, the ones wi' two names.

Oo needs two names, it's a pain in the skull,

Ah'd rather 'ave one name though some think it dull."

Says Barry to 'Arry after a long pause,

Cos it's 'ard for an Aardvark as 'e thinks of 'is words,

"Yeh, they scares me as well them Wildebeestes does,

Can they not jus' be 'appy wi' one name like we do,

Cos it mus' be real 'ard to choose one from the other.

Ma brain's sore already from thinkin' in two's,

Ah need to stop soon or Ah'll be in some bother."

So after a while, (it was nearly an hour),

They went for a drink in a pool of warm water.

One thing at a time in play or at work,

Is the best thing for Aardvarks'

So's their brains don't get 'urt.

CRITTERS

Out on the plain were some strange noisy critters,
They was loud an' was faster than Zebras an' others.
Much faster than Aardvarks but oo's in an' 'urry,
An 'urry's too much of a thing wot makes worry.

So it's rare fer an Aardvark to worry 'bout 'urry,
More rare fer an Aardvark to worry.
But like lots of things recent that 'Arry 'ad seen,
These critters were diff'rent from some wot 'ad been,
As big as a Gnu, an' as fast as 'em too,
An' ev'ry beast scattered as they ran straight through.

In the dust an' the noise they quickly came near,
showin' no sign of int'rest or fear.
"As puzzlin' a thing as 'as ever been seen."
Said 'Arry as the beasts disappeared in the green.

ABOUT THE AUTHOR

Martin has been writing silly poems for most of his life and he recently put some of them together as gift for his daughter Tori, who loves animals. His author wife, Soraya, was so impressed with the illustrations (rather than his sense of humour) that she insisted he should share his work.

Grown men and small boys will appreciate the words and most will appreciate his illustrations.

Made in the USA
Columbia, SC
18 April 2017